The First Words On Your Kid's Mind

POOPY PHONICS

by Jack, Jessica, and Kira Beiris

SIMAX

www.PoopyPhonics.com

First Printing, 2007

ISBN 0-9655109-6-4

P iS FoR POOP

OOP
OOP
OOP

LOOP
HOOP
GOOP
COOP
SNOOP

THIS IS A HULA _ _ _ _ _

1

EE EE EE
REMEMBER TO PEE

B E E
S E E
F E E
T E E

THIS IS A

_ _ _

2

You can say...

ART

ST**ART**

C**ART**

M**ART**

P**ART**

D**ART**

THIS IS A C _ _ _ _

But don't ever say...

FART

3

URP URP URP
I FEEL LIKE I GOTTA BURRRRRRP
SLURP
FURP
NURP
LURP
CURP
DURP
HURP
MURP

BUT BUT BUT, SOMETIMES YOU HAVE TO SAY ...

BUTT

UTT, UTT, UTT

MUTT
PUTT
HUT

NUT
RUT

THIS IS A

_ _ _

FLUSH

USH USH USH

USH

MUSH

BRUSH

CRUSH

HUSH

RUSH

BLUSH

Food goes SPLAT

FLAT
SLAT
SAT
MAT
RAT
FAT
HAT

10

Y is For Yuck

UCK
UCK
UCK

LUCK
BUCK
TRUCK
CLUCK

THIS IS A

_ _ _ _

What's that smell, nose?

ROSE
HOSE
CLOSE
POSE

OSE
OSE
OSE

THIS IS A _ _ _ _

S is For Slop

OP
OP
OP

TOP
FLOP
HOP
COP
MOP
POP

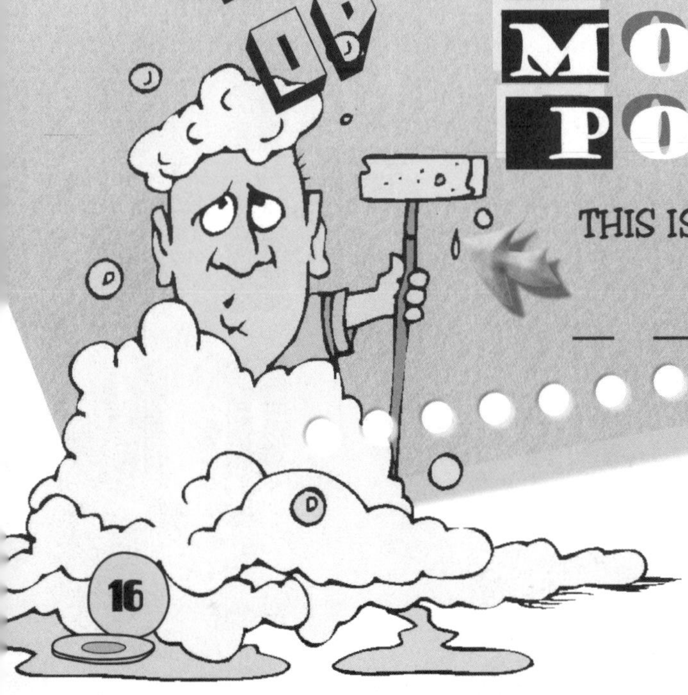

THIS IS A

___ ___ ___

SCUM
um um um um

S U M
H U M
G U M
M U M

AND DOES ANYTHING RHYME WITH BOOGER?

18

ARF
ARF
ARF

B IS FOR BARF

JUST

ARF OR SCARF

z

PIG

IG, IG, IG

FIG TWIG
BIG DIG
RIG WIG
JIG

THIS IS A

_ _ _ _ _

20

J IS FOR JUNK

UNK UNK UNK

FUNK HUNK

SKUNK DUNK

BUNK

AND HOW DO YOU SPELL...

THIS IS A

_ _ _ _ _

21

Don't be a SLOB

OB

JOB
KNOB
GOB
BLOB
SOB
MOB
ROB

THIS IS A DOOR..._ _ _ _ _

23

STICKY

PICKY

TRICKY

ICKY, ICKY, ICKY

25

SCAB

AB, AB, AB

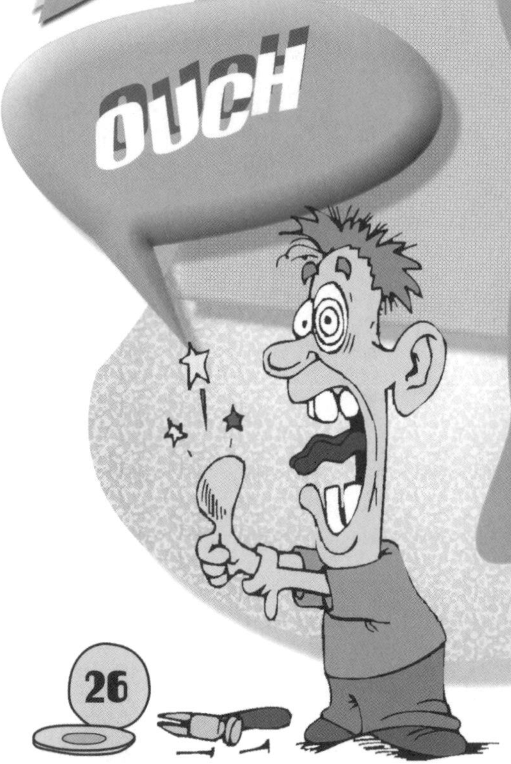

CAB
LAB
TAB
SLAB
STAB
BLAB
CRAB

STUFF

UFF
UFF
UFF

PUFF
GRUFF
HUFF
MUFF
BUFF
CUFF

THIS IS AN
EAR _ _ _ _

DROOL
OOL
OOL
OOL

P	OOL
C	OOL
T	OOL
SP	OOL
SCH	OOL

28

THIS IS A

_ _ _ _

UMP, UMP, UMP

RUMP
DUMP
SUMP
LUMP
PUMP
CLUMP
HUMP
JUMP

THIS IS A R _ _ _ _

And in the End there's a
TUSHY
USHY
USHY
USHY
PUSHY
MUSHY
BUSHY
CUSHY
THE END
30

POOP

Spread out a big pile of words and search for words

GOOP

Use as flashcards and retest just the hard ones

PUFF

Make fun sentences, on your own or as a challenge

HUFF

Tell a friend about PoopyPhonics.com

HOOP

Make fun sentences, on your own or as a challenge

BEE

Spread out a big pile of words and search for words

SNOOP

Don't tell anyone about PoopyPhonics.com

PEE

Use as flashcards and retest just the hard ones

32

CART

Spread out a big pile of words and search for words

DART

Use as flashcards and retest just the hard ones

START

Make fun sentences, on your own or as a challenge

FART

Don't tell anyone about PoopyPhonics.com

33

SNOT

Try to sort the words into rhyming piles

SLURP

Spread out a big pile of words and search for words

POT

Don't tell anyone about PoopyPhonics.com

BURP

Use as flashcards and retest just the hard ones

FAT

Spread out a big pile of words and search for words

RAT

Use as flashcards and retest just the hard ones

FLAT

Make fun sentences, on your own or as a challenge

SPLAT

Don't tell anyone about PoopyPhonics.com

DUCK

Make fun sentences, on your own or as a challenge

YUCK

Spread out a big pile of words and search for words

LUCK

Don't tell anyone about PoopyPhonics.com

TRUCK

Use as flashcards and retest just the hard ones

SEEK

Spread out a big pile of words and search for words

WEEK

Use as flashcards and retest just the hard ones

REEK

Make fun sentences, on your own or as a challenge

PEEK

Don't tell anyone about PoopyPhonics.com

37

WINK

Try to sort the words into rhyming piles

STINK

Spread out a big pile of words and search for words

PINK

Don't tell anyone about PoopyPhonics.com

INK

Use as flashcards and retest just the hard ones

CLOSE

Spread out a big pile of words and search for words

ROSE

Use as flashcards and retest just the hard ones

HOSE

Make fun sentences, on your own or as a challenge

NOSE

Don't tell anyone about PoopyPhonics.com

39

LIME

Make fun sentences, on your own or as a challenge

GRIME

Spread out a big pile of words and search for words

TIME

Don't tell anyone about PoopyPhonics.com

SLIME

Use as flashcards and retest just the hard ones

FLOP

Spread out a big pile of words and search for words

MOP

Use as flashcards and retest just the hard ones

POP

Make fun sentences, on your own or as a challenge

PLOP

Don't tell anyone about PoopyPhonics.com

41

HUM

Make fun sentences, on your own or as a challenge

MUM

Spread out a big pile of words and search for words

GUM

Don't tell anyone about PoopyPhonics.com

SCUM

Use as flashcards and retest just the hard ones

42

NUT

Spread out a big pile of words and search for words

MUTT

Use as flashcards and retest just the hard ones

BUTT

Make fun sentences, on your own or as a challenge

GOT

Don't tell anyone about PoopyPhonics.com

43

NOT

Don't tell anyone about PoopyPhonics.com

LOT

Make fun sentences, on your own or as a challenge

HOT

Use as flashcards and retest just the hard ones

ROT

Spread out a big pile of words and search for words

PIG

Spread out a big pile of words and search for words

ARF

Use as flashcards and retest just the hard ones

SCARF

Make fun sentences, on your own or as a challenge

BARF

Don't tell anyone about PoopyPhonics.com

45

PART

Make fun sentences, on your own or as a challenge

BIG

Spread out a big pile of words and search for words

TWIG

Don't tell anyone about PoopyPhonics.com

WIG

Use as flashcards and retest just the hard ones

46

IF

Spread out a big pile of words and search for words

RUSH

Use as flashcards and retest just the hard ones

SEE

Make fun sentences, on your own or as a challenge

MUSH

Don't tell anyone about PoopyPhonics.com

CRUSH

Make fun sentences, on your own or as a challenge

JUNK

Spread out a big pile of words and search for words

SKUNK

Don't tell anyone about PoopyPhonics.com

DUNK

Use as flashcards and retest just the hard ones

48

SOB

Spread out a big pile of words and search for words

BLOB

Use as flashcards and retest just the hard ones

GOB

Make fun sentences, on your own or as a challenge

SLOB

Don't tell anyone about PoopyPhonics.com

49

SNEEZE

Make fun sentences, on your own or as a challenge

FROM

Don't tell anyone about PoopyPhonics.com

SQUEEZE

Spread out a big pile of words and search for words

FREEZE

Use as flashcards and retest just the hard ones

PICKY

Spread out a big pile of words and search for words

TRICKY

Use as flashcards and retest just the hard ones

STICKY

Make fun sentences, on your own or as a challenge

ICKY

Don't tell anyone about PoopyPhonics.com

CRAB

Make fun sentences, on your own or as a challenge

CAB

Spread out a big pile of words and search for words

BLAB

Don't tell anyone about PoopyPhonics.com

SLAB

Use as flashcards and retest just the hard ones

52

BUFF

Spread out a big pile of words and search for words

OVER

Use as flashcards and retest just the hard ones

PUFF

Make fun sentences, on your own or as a challenge

STUFF

Don't tell anyone about PoopyPhonics.com

53

POOL

Try to sort the words into rhyming piles

COOL

Spread out a big pile of words and search for words

TOOL

Don't tell anyone about PoopyPhonics.com

DROOL

Use as flashcards and retest just the hard ones

LUMP

Spread out a big pile of words and search for words

JUMP

Use as flashcards and retest just the hard ones

RUMP

Make fun sentences, on your own or as a challenge

DUMP

Don't tell anyone about PoopyPhonics.com

BUSHY

Try to sort the words into rhyming piles

TUSHY

Spread out a big pile of words and search for words

CUSHY

Don't tell anyone about PoopyPhonics.com

MUSHY

Use as flashcards and retest just the hard ones

THE

Spread out a big pile of words and search for words

THE

Use as flashcards and retest just the hard ones

A

Make fun sentences, on your own or as a challenge

A

Don't tell anyone about PoopyPhonics.com

BUT

Make fun sentences, on your own or as a challenge

MOM

Spread out a big pile of words and search for words

OR

Don't tell anyone about PoopyPhonics.com

AND

Use as flashcards and retest just the hard ones

58

WAS

Spread out a big pile of words and search for words

WERE

Use as flashcards and retest just the hard ones

ARE

Make fun sentences, on your own or as a challenge

IS

Don't tell anyone about PoopyPhonics.com

HAVE

Make fun sentences, on your own or as a challenge

HAS

Spread out a big pile of words and search for words

HAD

Don't tell anyone about PoopyPhonics.com

WANTS

Use as flashcards and retest just the hard ones

DAD

Spread out a big pile of words and search for words

DID

Use as flashcards and retest just the hard ones

DOES

Make fun sentences, on your own or as a challenge

DO

Don't tell anyone about PoopyPhonics.com

NICE

Make fun sentences, on your own or as a challenge

BAD

Spread out a big pile of words and search for words

FUN

Don't tell anyone about PoopyPhonics.com

GOOD

Use as flashcards and retest just the hard ones

OUT

Spread out a big pile of words and search for words

IN

Use as flashcards and retest just the hard ones

FAST

Make fun sentences, on your own or as a challenge

SLOWLY

Don't tell anyone about PoopyPhonics.com

HE

Make fun sentences, on your own or as a challenge

YOU

Spread out a big pile of words and search for words

SHE

Don't tell anyone about PoopyPhonics.com

I

Use as flashcards and retest just the hard ones

64

HIM

Spread out a big pile of words and search for words

HER

Use as flashcards and retest just the hard ones

THEY

Make fun sentences, on your own or as a challenge

IT

Don't tell anyone about PoopyPhonics.com

NUMBER

Make fun sentences, on your own or as a challenge

OF

Spread out a big pile of words and search for words

ONE

Don't tell anyone about PoopyPhonics.com

WILL

Use as flashcards and retest just the hard ones

Spread out a big pile of words and search for words

TO

Use as flashcards and retest just the hard ones

OTHER

Make fun sentences, on your own or as a challenge

WAY

Don't tell anyone about PoopyPhonics.com

BY

WORD

Try to sort the words into rhyming piles

ABOUT

Spread out a big pile of words and search for words

PEOPLE

Don't tell anyone about PoopyPhonics.com

COULD

Use as flashcards and retest just the hard ones

THAN

Spread out a big pile of words and search for words

THEN

Use as flashcards and retest just the hard ones

MY

Make fun sentences, on your own or as a challenge

MANY

Don't tell anyone about PoopyPhonics.com

69

FIRST

Make fun sentences, on your own or as a challenge

WHAT

Spread out a big pile of words and search for words

THAT

Don't tell anyone about PoopyPhonics.com

THEM

Use as flashcards and retest just the hard ones

SO

Spread out a big pile of words and search for words

WATER

Use as flashcards and retest just the hard ones

THESE

Make fun sentences, on your own or as a challenge

ALL

Don't tell anyone about PoopyPhonics.com

SOME

Make fun sentences, on your own or as a challenge

BEEN

Spread out a big pile of words and search for words

CALL

Don't tell anyone about PoopyPhonics.com

WE

Use as flashcards and retest just the hard ones

YOUR

Spread out a big pile of words and search for words

FOR

Use as flashcards and retest just the hard ones

WHO

Make fun sentences, on your own or as a challenge

WHEN

Don't tell anyone about PoopyPhonics.com

CAN

Make fun sentences, on your own or as a challenge

WOULD

Spread out a big pile of words and search for words

MAKE

Don't tell anyone about PoopyPhonics.com

ON

Use as flashcards and retest just the hard ones

FIND

Spread out a big pile of words and search for words

LIKE

Use as flashcards and retest just the hard ones

SAID

Make fun sentences, on your own or as a challenge

NOW

Don't tell anyone about PoopyPhonics.com

LONG

Make fun sentences, on your own or as a challenge

AS

Spread out a big pile of words and search for words

WITH

Don't tell anyone about PoopyPhonics.com

THERE

Use as flashcards and retest just the hard ones

HIS

Spread out a big pile of words and search for words

DOWN

Use as flashcards and retest just the hard ones

INTO

Make fun sentences, on your own or as a challenge

USE

Don't tell anyone about PoopyPhonics.com

77

DAY

Try to sort the words into rhyming piles

TIME

Spread out a big pile of words and search for words

EACH

Don't tell anyone about PoopyPhonics.com

AN

Use as flashcards and retest just the hard ones

78

AT

Spread out a big pile of words and search for words

GET

Use as flashcards and retest just the hard ones

LOOK

Make fun sentences, on your own or as a challenge

WHICH

Don't tell anyone about PoopyPhonics.com

BE

Make fun sentences, on your own or as a challenge

TWO

Spread out a big pile of words and search for words

DO

Don't tell anyone about PoopyPhonics.com

COME

Use as flashcards and retest just the hard ones